Quirky, Jerky, Extra Perky

More about Adjectives

To Fiona

—B.P.C.

Adjective:
A word that describes a thing, idea, or living being

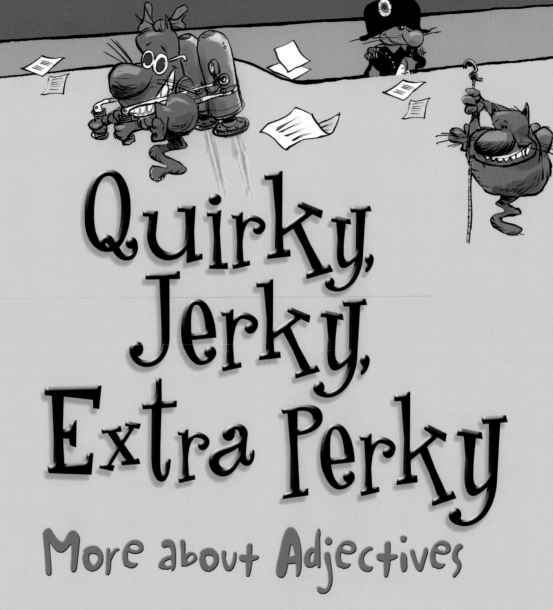

Quirky, Jerky, Extra Perky

More about Adjectives

by Brian P. Cleary

illustrations by Brian Gable

M MILLBROOK PRESS / MINNEAPOLIS

Adjectives
are words like yellow,
sleepy,
slumping,
somewhat mellow.

4

They give us lots of
great description,
like tall, left-handed,
young Egyptian.

They paint a picture using words,

like friendly dog
or baby birds,

Spotted, nearly rotted fruit, peppered eggs, and leopard suit.

See how these words
tell us more?
A wild goat,
a mild boar.

8

Particulars are what you give
each time you use an
adjective.

London's often **cool**
and *clammy*.

Humid best describes Miami.

Cold's a handy adjective
if Greenland is the place you live.

Like wrinkled hands and crinkled pliers,

adjectives are modifiers,

telling more about the noun,
like crazy cat or lazy clown.

Kind of quirky,

extra perky,

quite polite,

or slightly jerky.

Woolen socks, a knitted shawl—

adjectives describe them all!

Like sly,

sarcastic,

so fantastic,

enthusiastic, and elastic,

adjectives make phrases sing

and keep our language interesting!

A wilted rose, a chartreuse vase, a cheery, kind, and florid face.

Music that's soothing,
soup that is steaming,

Served in a bowl that's
so bright that it's gleaming.

Adjectives tell us
when someone is serious,
fearless or frightened
or even delirious.

Like, "Hear the mysterious bat
as it screeches."
See how exciting this fun part of speech is?

They modify nouns
in ways that explain
if a movie is brilliant,
bizarre, or inane.

Because we have
adjectives,
we get to pick
words like crumbled and red
when describing
a brick.

We can say that it's simple

or scary
or splendid,

describing the skating
 that Mary or Glen did.

They help us picture
lots of things
When we can't
really see 'em.

Yes, **adjectives**
help make our mind
a kind of **art** museum!

They've told us of a doughnut that was round and plump and sprinkled.

The winking stars above us as they've sparkled and they've twinkled.

The sour apple candies from the cozy corner store.

Adjectives help tell us about all these things and more!

So, what is an adjective?
Do you know?

ABOUT THE AUTHOR & ILLUSTRATOR

BRIAN P. CLEARY is the author of the best-selling Words Are CATegorical® series, as well as the Math Is CATegorical®, Food Is CATegorical™, Animal Groups Are CATegorical™, Adventures in Memory™, and Sounds Like Reading® series. He has also written Do You Know Dewey? Exploring the Dewey Decimal System, Six Sheep Sip Thick Shakes: And Other Tricky Tongue Twisters, and several other books. Mr. Cleary lives in Cleveland, Ohio.

BRIAN GABLE is the illustrator of several Words Are CATegorical® books and the Math Is CATegorical® series. Mr. Gable also works as a political cartoonist for the Globe and Mail newspaper in Toronto, Canada.

Text copyright © 2007 by Brian P. Cleary
Illustrations copyright © 2007 by Lerner Publishing Group, Inc.

Millbrook Press
A division of Lerner Publishing Group, Inc.
241 First Avenue North
Minneapolis, MN 55401 U.S.A.

Website address: www.lernerbooks.com

Library of Congress Cataloging-in-Publication Data

Cleary, Brian P., 1959-
   Quirky, jerky, extra perky : more about adjectives / by Brian P. Cleary ;
illustrations by Brian Gable.
      p. cm. — (Words are categorical)
   ISBN 978-0-8225-6709-7 (lib. bdg. : alk. paper)
   ISBN 978-1-58013-695-3 (eBook)
   1. English language—Adjective—Juvenile literature. I. Gable, Brian, 1949-
II. Title. III. Series: Cleary, Brian P., 1959- Words are categorical.
PE1241.C58 2007
428.2—dc22   2006010756

Manufactured in China
9-41682-5535-3/23/2016